An Original Model Creating A New Global Structure

By

Veryl Yoder

"An Original Model Creating
A New Global Structure"
By Veryl Yoder

Printed in the USA

ISBN: 9798864475775

An Original Model Creating A New Global Structure

DEDICATION

I would like to dedicate this book to Kristy Hotchkiss

A tremendous, high-quality person who

supported me throughout the year.

CONTENTS

An Original Model Creating A New Global Structure

An Original Model Creating A New Global Structure

ACKNOWLEDGMENTS

I want to acknowledge the Amish community.

From the insights I received from them.

TELEOL0GICAL

The Teleological Views of Veryl Yoder

The following are my efforts at classifying the myriad patterns of social, religious, psychological, and political thought, behavior, and organization of societies in our world. In broad sweeps, I see some cultures that emphasize collectivity more as differentiated from those that emphasize individualism. Likewise, I see differentiation between those emphasizing an analytical approach to social organization, highlighting the material world in the scientific and technical realms. On the other hand, those embody a more synthetic approach that emphasizes an immaterial, spiritual dimension.

The Universal Model

Analytical Collective

(symbol: large triangle)

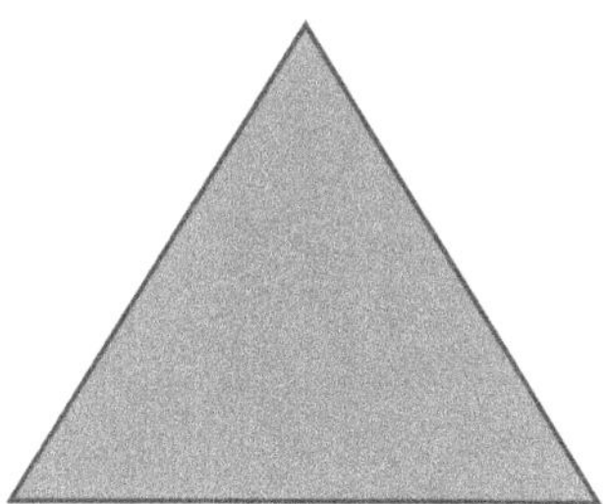

"High context" societies (group cultural identity)

Fascism

Patriarchal

Strong sense of identity Science & Technology

Productivity

Rigid morality Chain of command Theocracy

Choleric temperament

Islam (Wahhabi Islam)

A God-given sense of belonging

Group Cultural Identity

Synthetic Collective

(symbol: large circle)

"High context societies"

Healthy sex, marriage, family Community values

Buddhism

Amish

Melancholy temperament

Communism – Community – Family - Individual

Self-worth between Family and community includes a

bonding between Children and Parents.

Then, a horizontal connection between

Individual & Community.

Spiritual Self-worth

Here are some thoughts on spiritual self-worth. The essence of the two spiritualities is the same, approached differently with varying technologies and terminologies. There is a discussion of the fruit of the spirit in Galatians chapter 5 and Corinthians 13. Love is the subject of this chapter. These traits are synonymous with self-worth. When Western Christians talk about peace with God and Eastern spirituality, They talk about being centered and at one with the universe. When Western Christians practice personal devotions, Bible reading and prayer, and Eastern spiritual talks about meditation, using self-worth interchangeably with self-confidence is a mistake. Self-confidence is obtained by learning and accomplishing different things. Being overly confident can lead to arrogance. Arrogance is pride and superiority based on its inferiority. True self-worth is not superiority based on. Inferiority, but rather accurate. Humility. True self-worth is also not cheap.

Superficial self-esteem, as portrayed in families and educational circles, has all participated in the entitlement age surrounding youth and adolescence. When a handsome male is the high school quarterback, and a beautiful female is the most popular cheerleader, they may possess Self-esteem. But not true self-worth. True self-worth originates from deep within, at an early age, from being connected first with parents, family, and friends. Friends must not be superficial, and then their relationships feel a solid connection to each other. If one does not obtain self-worth early, one can bring it later by receiving healing & wholeness. Meditation and feeling connected to persons and spiritual groups must (nurture synthetic), salvation, and authentic self-worth. Please respond with your affirmation and insights.

It is a total mistake to use self-worth interchangeably with self-confidence. Self-confidence is obtained by learning and accomplishing different things. Being overconfident can lead to arrogance, pride, and superiority based on inferiority. However, genuine humility also comes at a price, requiring a deep self-worth. Superficial self-esteem is portrayed in families and educational circles, particularly in this entitlement age surrounding youth and adolescence. A handsome male, the school's quarterback, and a beautiful female cheerleader can have high self-esteem simultaneously.

Nevertheless, true self-worth does not exist. The source of true self-worth lies deep within. Early in life, both individuals are connected to their parents and families. Their friends weren't superficial in their relationships and had felt a strong connection to each other. If one does not obtain self-worth early, one may receive it later through healing (wholeness and synthetic) salvation.

Analytical Individual

(symbol: small triangle)

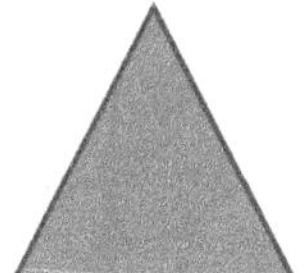

"Low context" societies Democratic capitalism

Judea-Christian Personal salvation

Charismatic Evangelical,

Individual morality

Sanguine temperament

Synthetic Individual

(symbol: small circle)

"Low context" societies

Democratic-socialism Spiritual mysticism Matriarchy

Peace & Justice Hinduism

(National Council of Churches) Phlegmatic temperament

Descriptions of the Four Categories of Thought and Social Organization

Analytical Collective

The Analytical Collective takes the form of a vertical hierarchy. It reflects a secular political structure, sometimes in hierarchical organizations such as the military or police force. It is often antithetical to a communitarian, spiritual form of social organization. Emphasizes dogma, doctrine, creeds, and ideologies. It is often associated with dictatorial governments or fascism.

Strengths: Answers the need for identity. The result is productivity—discipline, and order in society.

Weaknesses: Power and control. Prejudice. Oppression. War. Violence. Racism. Militant fundamentalism & fanaticism.

Analytical Individual

Reflects the need for privatization in our religious, political, and economic organization of society. Strong emphasis on personal salvation, personal morality, and private enterprise. Emphasizes pietism. Sometimes, it relies on incentives and rewards. It is often associated with a democratic government.

Strengths: Personal growth, spiritually speaking. Personal economic prosperity but not the accumulation of wealth.

Weaknesses: Accumulation of personal wealth. Greed and materialism. Unrestrained capitalism.

Synthetic Collective

Reflects an abstract form of thinking in the spiritual sense, which is horizontal inter-connectedness. Emphasizes an egalitarian merging and fusing of individuals into one collective whole.

Strengths: Spiritual growth within the community. Achievement without concern for status.

Weaknesses: Aspiring for cultural and educational status.

Synthetic Individual

Reflects the need for individual and human dignity and worth with a humanitarian emphasis. Often characteristic of representative democracies or democratic socialism.

Strengths: Individual mystic, religious experience. Dealing with inner harmony and balance, religiously speaking. Stresses individual autonomy.

Weaknesses: Super hedonism with a need for self-gratification in a materialistic, luxurious environment.

Integration Of The Psychological World View With The Spiritual World View

(This thesis was articulated to a friend as we gathered together at the Monk's Tunic, an erstwhile cafe in Lancaster City. Therefore, I call it the "Monk's Tunic Thesis."

This thesis depicts the relationship between Adler's "identity" and the concept of "self-worth."

Terms "Power," "No. 1," "Distinctive," "Unique," and "Original" can be interchanged with the concept of superiority. One's cultural or social identity or ethnic background can be a form of superiority or inferiority.

"Cultural & Social Identity"

When the terms "superior" and "inferior" meet in the
middle, that middle would be utopia
from a relative perspective.

Superior

———

———

Alder's will to power------------------Freud's will to pleasure

———

———

Inferior

When the terms "superior" and "inferior" meet in the middle,
that middle would be utopia from a relative perspective.

Chakras

Eastern Relativity

		Adlerian	Freudian
B Cognition Is Dominant			
Perfect Balance	Level 7 / Level 6		
Power to Influence For the Good	Level 5		
Agape	Level 4		
D Cognition Is Dominant			
Phileo	Level 3	Power for the sake of power.	Promiscuous Sex
Power is "Power Over" Physical Control	Level 2	Corruption/ Abuse of power	Prostitution Rape
Base Level	Level 1	War/Class Oppression Glorify militarism's	Crime

Key phrase: Uniqueness and identity are inevitable but are relative in direct proportion to D-cognition versus Power, which is a form of identity but a distorted form of identity. It's the norm in our society.

Maslow's Process Of Self-Actualization

During the last 2000 years, the Hegelian dialectic has been off balance concerning Adlerian thought and balance of power. We have accepted power and war, though we say promiscuous sex is wrong.

That's off balance.

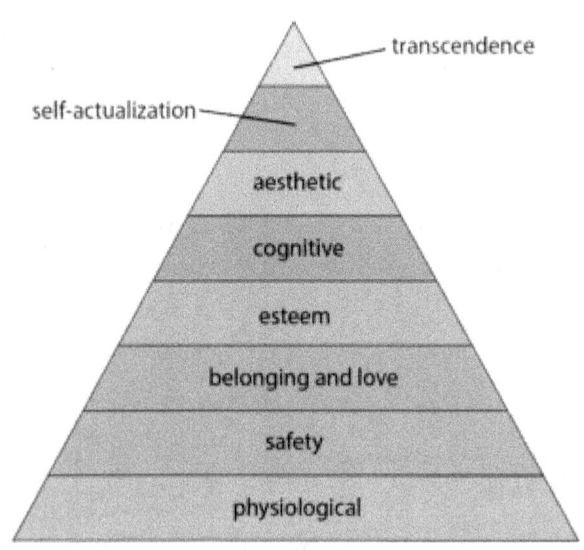

Maslow's Hierarchy of Needs

Self-worth = Agape love   (interchangeable)

Inferiority = Lack of self-worth

Cognition = awareness motivation

D-cognition & deficiency motivation

B-cognition = agape love: agape love = self-worth (on levels 4, 5, 6)

D-cognition is predominant on Levels 1, 2 & 3, but B-cognition is also present, though sub-dominant. There is the "spark of the divine" even at those levels.

The transition from Level 3 to Level 4 is a significant shift.

Level 4
B-cognition becomes dominant
D-cognition becomes sub-dominate
Level 4 is realistic and attainable for life today.

Level 5
B-Cognition increases. D-cognition decreases. (and so on up)

Levels 6&7
Level 7 - the lower self is completely gone.

Society today is basically on Level 3, where promiscuous sex and power are the norm.

Children must be nurtured with a deep sense of self-worth for healthy development and social relationships to emerge later.

From Adlerian thought, even the material causes of war, e.g., oil greed, are based on allegiance to our country and peoplehood identity. There is a close link between identity and self-worth.

There is a strong need for both identity and self-worth. If a leader has as strong a sense of group cultural identity but no sense of self-worth, that leader will take the collective identity and throw it out of perspective in the leader's struggle for self-worth. Conversely, suppose a leader has a strong sense of self- worth but no group collective identity. In that case, that leader will also conquer to achieve cultural identity because of the need to belong.

International Implications Of This Model Are Based On The Theory Of Self-Worth.

The U.S. has an identity, an ideology of "freedom and democracy," but has the problem of low self-worth, hence the need to be superior and the drive to control others. {One can appreciate much in the United States but oppose its imperialism, which stems from its lack of self-worth.)

Extremist Muslims could also have a strong cultural identity but have a problem with self-worth. Amish have a group cultural identity and also a strong sense of self-worth.

Muslim cultures have advantages over the West because of their strong cultural identity.

The West is based on individualism, but the East is on a robust collective model. {It is possible to synthesize East and West.)

"High context" cultures are more common in the Middle East, Asia, and the global South than in Europe and countries with low racial diversity. "Low context" cultures are more common in Australia, England, Canada, Germany, Ireland, New Zealand, Scandinavian countries, Switzerland, and the United States.

Mystic's From The East & West

Synthesize East & West

Eastern mystic - Aurobindo

a. Synthetic Collective
b. Synthetic Individual
c. Analytical Individual

Western mystic - Teilhard de Chardin

a. Analytical Individual
b. Analytical Collective
c. Synthetic Collective

Analytical Collective:
Science and technology
(temptation for power dictatorship)

Analytical Individual:
Capitalism
(individual morality)

Synthetic Collective:
Holistic interdependence
(interaction of family & community)
Including sex & marriage.

Synthetic individual:
Mystical Spirituality

All these categorizations must be considered from the standpoint of proportionate combinations containing degrees of concentration within a context of unifying opposites.

Power is a form of identity, albeit a distorted form. The proper identity arrangement is God's love (very abstract), a religious identity with a group identity with family. Group identity creates self-worth, which provides a basis for true spirituality. True fulfillment, e.g., Amish or non-jihadist Muslim, comes from God within the context of the collective group.

Muslims with strong cultural identity and a strong sense of family and community have an advantage over the West. Muslim theocracy is terrible since it stresses power without a strong sense of self-worth.

When I speak of Islamic culture, I am certainly not advocating the jihadist or terrorist aspect of Islam. Nor am I talking about the weakness of Islamic culture, such as the oppression of women. Instead, I am talking about moderate Islam and the correlation of abstract dynamics as a strength.

When I look at the abstract dynamics of moderate Islam, I correlate it with an Eastern cultural model of the Synthetic

Collective. This needs to be viewed from the standpoint of a subdivision within my universal model.

As society moves toward the ideal of the Synthetic Collective, it still may choose to incorporate elements of the Synthetic Individual {such as human rights and democratic values) and the Analytical Collective as well.

"High context" and "low context" societies tend to see ideals of social organization differently. High-context institutions tend to value the collective more than the individual.

High Context Societies

They may prioritize their goals in this order:

Synthetic Collective (prioritizing human relationships)

Analytical Collective (group cultural identity)

Synthetic Individual (democratic values)

Analytical Individual (financial freedom, micro-finance)

Low Context Societies

They may have a reverse priority:

Analytical Individual (technology and financial productivity)

Synthetic Individual {democratic values)

Analytical Collective {group cultural identity)

Synthetic Collective {high context relationships)

The Western analytical perspective is essential to the betterment of the world. It is crucial because economic productivity and science and technology are married. This marriage results in productivity, problem-solving, and progress. An example of that could be illustrated in medical science and technology advancement.

The West needs to be innovative in that it retains its strengths but counteracts its weakness of status and extreme individualism with some form of the collective.

Amish have a strong sense of self-worth from God, being committed to God and each other. Tourists see this in the faces of the Amish.

The West is based on status and power for identity. In the northeast U.S., you lay out your "cards": the car you drive, your educational degrees, your university, your house, your job ... and the strongest suit of cards wins.

Liberal U.S. Mennonites correlate with European socialism.

Though Freud tended to analyze everything through sex drive, people's sense of identity (as per Adler) is as powerful as sexual drive. The purpose of group identity is just as strong as the need to propagate the species. In actuality, the importance of Adler vs. Freud is 50 / 50.

When the U.S. (the West) goes to other countries and projects a sense of superiority, they're missing the mark completely. When the U.S. embodies science, aptitude, and productivity, that's what the West has to contribute for the good of the world. Americans think of a market economy (analytical individual) and democracy (synthetic individual). Americans have no sense of the collective.

At this point in history, Islam has an advantage over the West due to the paradigm shift moving towards the collective. However, the West still has something to contribute to science and technology.

Now, the world needs to come together in a synthesis of the Hegelian dialectic.

The paradigm about the collective can be illustrated in that the world is evolving toward a holistic world community. This is based on the (Hegelian) synthetic dynamic in general. This can be shown in the difference between the parochial, analytical United States and the holistic, synthetic United Nations. The UN dynamic is the basis for a holistic world community.

The jihadist has a strong group collective identity but little sense of self-worth. The West makes them feel inferior, so they think they must fight for that self-worth. American imperialism has no intention of group collective identity while lacking self-worth. This leads to their need to feel superior to others. The paradigm shift is moving toward the collective and can be illustrated in another manner using this universal model. There needs to be a move from the individual to the collective. The individual would be the Analytical Individual (democratic capitalism) and the Synthetic Individual (democratic socialism). The move toward the collective would involve the Analytical and Synthetic Collective. The Analytical Collective would include group cultural identity, and the Synthetic Collective would consist of high-context culture. At the present moment, on the world stage, the US, the West, and Israel need to take a step back on the world stage. There needs to be mutual respect between collective non-Western cultures and individualistic Western cultures.

There must be a 50-50 balance between Western and non-western cultures. In the same way, there needs to be a 50-50 balance between the material, scientific, and immaterial spiritual. Teleological is a good term because it involves a developmental process moving toward a final climax.

Eventually, western, low-context culture with its pros will be synthesized with non-Western context society and its pros. When the context drops from both the Low context west and the high context non-west, this will result in a perfect balance from a relative perspective. The result will be a utopian society.

Implications For Peacemaking

1. We must recognize that Islamic culture has something essential to contribute to the world.

2. The US needs a stronger sense of belonging and group cultural identity, with a balanced patriotism. We need less individualism. First, we must admit where we're wrong. We cannot think of ourselves as superior. American exceptionalism has to go, but it should not be anti-Americanism. There must be mutual respect between the East and the West. Both sides have something to contribute to the world. Now, both sides are at fault, but especially American imperialism. American imperialism must be dealt with before progress can be made. Greed: at the root of greed is a struggle for superiority. Greed is the result of seeking identity.

We need a world government with representatives from each country. We need genuinely selfless representation. We must develop the sense of the collective by emphasizing small groups throughout the country. Goodwill will overcome evil because so many people will work at it.

Some of these ideas may appear contradictory, but the pictures are highly abstract and need to be viewed from the standpoint of proportionate combinations with the context of unifying opposites.

Addendum 10/27/2016, 3/19/2017

Analytical

Dualism-Heaven or Hell

Synthetic

Relativism, Evolution within Gradations of an Indivisible After-Life (Universal Salvation).

As I mentioned before, the dynamics of the Analytical need to be applied to the Material (Scientific-Technical), and the dynamics of the Synthetic need to be applied to the Immaterial-Spiritual.

ABOUT THE AUTHOR

Veryl Yoder is a promising author and a prolific wordsmith. He continues highlighting a remarkable versatility in writing style. The author's commitment to social justice and advocacy for marginalized communities is evident in their non-fiction works, which tackle pressing societal issues with empathy and insight.

In addition to their writing, the author is an active mentor to aspiring writers, generously sharing their knowledge and experience to nurture the next generation of literary talent.